The Art of the Siesta

The Art of the Siesta

Thierry Paquot

Translated from the French by Ken Hollings

First published in Great Britain and the United States in 2003 by
MARION BOYARS PUBLISHERS LTD
24 Lacy Road, London SW15 1NL

www.marionboyars.co.uk

Distributed in Australia and New Zealand by Peribo Pty Ltd,
58 Beaumont Road, Kuring-gai, NSW 2080

10 9 8 7 6 5 4 3 2 1

Originally published in 1998 by Editions Zulma,
under the title *L'Art de la sieste*
© Editions Zulma, 1998
© This translation, Ken Hollings, 2003

A CIP catalogue record for this book is available from the British Library.
A CIP catalog record for this book is available from the Library of Congress.

ISBN 0-7145-3092-1

Set in Sabon 11/14
Printed and bound by in the UK by Bookmarque, London

Preliminaries

From one siesta comes another...

Irise slowly from my desk and switch off my computer. I head towards my bed, take off my shoes, socks and trousers, unplug the phone and bring a regretful halt to Martine Geliot's *Récital de Harpe*. Then I stretch out, close my eyes and hear myself wishing the empty room and my own self 'sweet dreams' in tones that are almost inaudible, like a murmur, a caress. A few seconds later, and I am no longer in control. I am entirely 'elsewhere', in sleep's domain... What time is it? Just before one-thirty. The beginning of the afternoon: that brief yet so agreeable moment when the siesta calls and you're not sure how to respond. By sleeping? When there's so much to do? Sleeping? You can't be serious! And if someone should hear about this and pass it on to my associates, my students, colleagues and superiors...? *'No, no. Don't disturb me. I'm taking time out. I'm not in to anyone. I'm sleeping!' What? Oh yes! 'Thierry Paquot has gone bye-byes, like a little baby!'* Shame on him. Shame on all who give themselves up to this practice from another century, which should be denounced, forbidden, punished! Daytime is daytime. Good God, it's meant for work! And the night...the night? That's when you sleep. End of story. No argument. No excuses. It's altogether an excellent arrangement: judicious, rational and beneficial to all. Everyone knows where they are: both employer and employee. In short, it's unreasonable to withdraw from social life just to snatch a quick nap, as if it were a mere nothing! All the same, whenever I'm confronted with this kind of argument from responsible individuals, I have to admit, confess and even proclaim that the siesta is a high point in an art of living – yes, an art of living! – that should be defended, popularized and practised with both joy and solemnity. Men and women of all ages, of every latitude and time-zone, of every profession, assert your individuality and resist planetary time, satellite time, totalitarian time! This is only the beginning, the siesta marches on...

The siesta is an imperative. It forces itself upon you more than it entreats. It's simply there, seductive, alluring and tender: in a word, irresistible. It enfolds you in its warmth, cajoles you and coaxes you. You follow blindly. Despite yourself, you close your eyes and relax. Your body, which was weighing you down just a moment before, now seems progressively lighter, invisible, non-existent. Happiness – or a form of happiness – overwhelms you. Let yourself be, let yourself go and, with surprise, surrender yourself. To what? A new master? Or mistress? Little conspirator... are you trying to hide an illicit liaison? Yes, an assignation in broad daylight – disapproved of by productive morality – with the night, with Hypnos... The siesta requires you to enter into an agreement with diurnal sleep, paying homage to it, staying in its company, leaving the door open to dreaming... The siesta is a gift.

The child is agitated. He cries and bawls, rolls around on the floor, knocks over everything in his way, refusing to go to sleep. The proposition seems so menacing to him, almost like a punishment. To calm him, you must take him in your arms, wrap all of your love around him and accompany him into sleep, mingling his anxieties and fears with your own pleasure in resting. Rest should follow a meal, however frugal or substantial. Upon waking, the child will be better disposed towards a world that he regards once again with an unrestrained appetite. The siesta is like a pause for breath, a necessary moment in which to recover one's strength and one's spirit. The baby and the young child are also nurtured by this unique and precious moment: the siesta. The sleeping infant is even more beautiful. Look at him. He exudes peace. The sleeping infant resembles a calm and radiant landscape. A snowbound landscape in which all sound is muffled and where, through its reverberation, the silence sings.

A sunlit landscape in which the sinews are warmed and dreaming is invoked. More than one painter has brought about the 'artialization' of the landscape, as Montaigne expressed it so well. In fact, a landscape painting teaches us how to look at and appreciate 'Nature' better. It's a similar question of 'artializing' sleep so that we can share its respiration, its serenity and its enchanting half-shadows. May the act of falling asleep lead us out of the darkness and into glades which, whether laughing or in torment, are always illuminated...

I

Depictions of the Siesta

Look closely at the Infant Jesus in the *Madonna del Silenzio* by Domenico Zampiere, otherwise known as Domenichino. Although not posed in a manner that would lend itself to sleep, a communicable sense of quiet emanates from him. His mother holds her index finger up to her lips, inviting her guests to cease their commotion. 'Hush,' she whispers. 'The child is sleeping...'

Giorgione, a contemporary of Domenichino, painted a *Sleeping Venus*, which he never finished, the plague in Venice carrying him off to an eternal siesta. Titian completed the interrupted painting, adding certain details to the landscape and taking care of the sky, not touching the naked young woman, whose left hand nestles delicately between her thighs. Is she resting after the delicious tensions of masturbation? The drapery upon which she reclines speaks of disarray in repose. During the same period, at the very start of the sixteenth century, Piero di Cosimo painted a *Venus, Mars and Cupid* (1505): except it is Mars who sleeps, stretched out naked in the middle of a joyful landscape, filled with animals and cherubs.

Caravaggio's *Rest during the Flight into Egypt* expresses the feeling of relaxation that the siesta provides, because that's exactly what it's about. Madonna and Child are sleeping while a young male angel plays on his violin the partita that Joseph holds up to him. Music also plays its part amid the calmness and respite. Fear has no place is this brief hiatus; the reasons for flight and the uncertainties of the chase are forgotten for a moment, while a certain serenity lingers, covering the participants with an invisible protective veil. The child fears nothing. What worries could he have, lulled by the sweet breath of his mother? Orazio Gentileschi's *Rest during the Flight into Egypt* (1622) has Joseph plunged into a deep sleep, while Mary fights to keep her eyelids open. Jesus, still awake, is feeding, casting about him the baleful glance of one who does not wish to be disturbed during so agreeable a union, so joyful a suckling.

In *The Harvest*, as well as in *The Land of Cocagne*, Pieter Bruegel the Elder shows men collapsed either from their labours or a plentiful meal: asleep, legs splayed out, without the slightest embarrassment but with communicable feelings of pleasure... The 'Land of Cocagne' does not exist. No road leads to it except for that of the imagination. The historian Jean Delumeau[1], who has visited more than one Land of Cocagne from Boccaccio to Rabelais, tells us that they all possess rivers of honey, fountains of wine and trees whose fruits grow back as soon as they are picked; it rains legs of mutton, the mountains are made of 'grated parmesan cheese', and roast suckling pigs run about, the knife with which to carve them already in their skin. In short, they are regions where the living is made easy for those who are in need, those who can barely survive in a world bruised by war and torn by inequalities and injustices of every kind... Faced with the growing weight of misfortunes pressing down upon him, the poor wretch takes refuge in anticipating a better world, in descriptions of a 'Land of Cocagne'. The picture's original title 'Luilekkerland' translates literally as 'The Land of Nice Things', so it's hardly surprising to find depictions of pies, cakes, roast chickens etc... This dream of abundance, rest and indolence is a response to the famine that hangs constantly over the countryside. This is what Bruegel the Elder's renowned painting conveys to us through its colours and postures and pantomime. It offers us a sliver of consolation, a hope. The soldier, the peasant and the student (there is a book lying beside him) who figure in this painting have certainly eaten well – for once. Above all, however, they represent a response to the widespread poverty and pestilence and the pains of war. Sometimes, while studying a reproduction of *The Harvest*, I can hear the reaper's measured snoring and

I smile with pleasure, both on his behalf and as tribute to the comfort and peace conferred on me by the age and the society in which I live and sleep. Strange, isn't it? How agreeable it is to enter a picture where no one expects you: as if you were breaking in. There you are in your up-to-date clothes and with the perceptions of your own time, questioning such and such a person, as if this 'other world' were familiar to you. It's true that the simple routine of the siesta is enough to admit you into the happy company of these fine fellows, who remind you of Alexander the Blessed. Have you ever walked into a film, like the heroine of Woody Allen's *The Purple Rose of Cairo*? It's funny, but I get the impression that the siesta encourages this type of journey... To elide a painting with a scene from a film, to superimpose images upon reality, to give space to whatever may arise, to bring into motion that which sensibly remains still; this is the magic of encroaching sleep... But let us return to our private gallery, where we had reached Bruegel. Almost a century later, other Flemish painters were paying homage to the siesta, or at least that's the feeling I get from some of their canvasses, even if this interpretation is biased. *The Kermis* by Rubens sweeps me up in a wild dance, but this doesn't prevent one couple from lying down upon the grass in each other's arms before caressing one another and falling into a restorative sleep. Rembrandt's *Philosopher in Meditation* (1632) is certainly 'thinking', isolating himself in a dark corner of the room in order to do so. Having sought out this solitude, he inclines his head, closes his eyes and goes in search of ideas...but is he sleeping? I think so. 'Half-asleep', he leaves this world behind him and, at his leisure, wanders, muses, dreams, constructs theories, engages with other thinkers and elaborates upon new ideas. So too has Carel Fabritius' *The Sentry* deserted his post for sleep. Only a small dog remains awake, watching with tenderness – with 'humanity' – over the young soldier recouping his strength. As for Jan Steen's *Couple in Bed*, even though it depicts a scene in a brothel, nothing will prevent me from placing it at siesta time or from imagining that, after some agreeable caresses, sleep will tenderly envelope the couple, like the blanket that covers them, and keep them warm.

In *The Sleep of Endymion* (1792), Anne-Louis Girodet-Trioson portrays a blessed soul who is breathing so calmly, so peacefully and so softly that you can hardly hear him... He might be mistaken for an angel, were it not for his sex, which also lies sleeping, coiled within the shelter of his pubic undergrowth.

The many courtesans and bathers, prostitutes and mannequins that populate the canvasses of Orientalists, Impressionists, Pointillists, Fauves etc. are as indolent as they are active at their siestas. *Woman Caressing a Parrot* (1827) by Eugène Delacroix endows the siesta with colours that are hot, carnal, erotic. His *Women of Algiers in Their Apartment* (1834) leaves to the imagination the preparations required for a dream-filled siesta: the tobacco in their hookah being, it's true, an amenable method of transport...

Gustave Courbet's *Young Women on the Banks of the Seine* (1857) seem preoccupied. One of them is thinking of nothing. She even appears sullen: is she bored? The other is fast asleep. The two seem distant with one another, as opposed to the female lovers Courbet was commissioned to paint for the Turkish collector Khalil Bey in *Sleep* (1866), none of whose details suggest that it's about a siesta at all. Tenderly entwined, the two lesbians are united in a shared sleep after making love. Khalil Bey is the same man who bought Courbet's *The Origin of the World* and who also acquired *Le Bain Turc* (1862), that famous circular canvas, 108cm in diameter, painted by Jean Auguste Dominique Ingres. As if through a keyhole, the painting draws us into the harem, where naked women brush against each other, converse... Some are awake; others sleep. Some 'pose' while others stifle a yawn. One strums an instrument while gazing at two young women. Is she playing a tune from their native land? The painter does not make you hear it; he makes you see it – the abandoning of time to the siesta, which is nothing but an awakening of senses. That, at least, is how I see it. In the innumerable '*déjeuners sur l'herbe*' of which the period seems fond, we find individuals surrendering themselves, or just about to surrender themselves, to the siesta. In *Bathers at Asnières* (1884) as in *A Sunday on La Grande Jatte* (1884-6), Seurat argues the case for 'the right to a siesta' in an age when resting at home was not open to all. It's true that the workers preferred to keep Mondays sacred, leaving Sunday to the pious... Manet, Monet, Toulouse-Lautrec, Gaugin and many others have depicted that 'arrested passage of time', that break in the day, that 'time to oneself' which is the siesta. It would never form the central theme or title of a painting, but its presence is indisputable. Often the painter lets it be known that the siesta accompanies sexuality, physical desire and the coupling of bodies. Things were different for Edouard Vuillard's women, shown reclining upon a day-bed or couch: *Misia and Thadée Natanson* (1897); *Woman Sitting in a Garden* and *Woman Reading in a Garden* (both 1898); *Madame Hessel on the Sofa* (1910-1912). Women with their eyes fixed upon a book or lost in inaccessible dreaming, like butterflies in flight. Nevertheless they are taking a siesta: a waking siesta on occasion, since it does not demand total relaxation, complete absence or exile. The siesta can be practised in a thousand and one ways: either by falling into a heavy sleep, dozing for a handful of minutes or by emptying one's mind for a few seconds... In the company of painters, the siesta adorns itself with all the colours of an accommodating palette. And you who fall asleep, however quickly, pay attention to the brief prelude that announces the coming of sleep itself. It is here that you can create your own pictures, from derivations to valued canvasses. You flow into them. Everything becomes coloured in a composition that is certainly symbolic but indescribable and of impenetrable significance. There are deep yellow siestas, when it is hot and you are enveloped in sweat. There are red siestas: violent and incendiary. There are white siestas: virginal, pure and light. There are siestas buffeted by sandstorms, capricious seas and garrulous winds. Coloured siestas are the best. Pacifying and tormenting at the same time, they are irreplaceable.

II

The Midday Demon

In two successive editions of the *Revue de l'Histoire des Religions*[2] and in two issues of the *Revue des études slaves*[3] Roger Caillois published the abstract for his thesis on Religious Science. Its subject: the *Midday Demons*. In it, he tackled a hitherto little explored continent that Antiquity had populated with demons, sirens, satyrs, nymphs and other terrifying creatures of the imagination... The *midday demon* represents the trouble which can overwhelm certain individuals at midday. Why the 'sixth hour' more than any other? It's the easiest to recognize: the one moment of the day when shadows are hardly seen, and the sun is at its triumphant height. For the Greeks, and then later the Romans, this anomaly owes its origins to a specific designation – *meridies* in Latin – in just the same way that 'midnight' signifies 'the middle of the night'. To be precise, the Latin verb '*meridiari*' means 'to take a siesta', and the English word 'meridian' is derived from the Latin '*meridianus*', meaning 'of, or pertaining, to midday' and can be used as an adjective as in the expression 'the midday devil', which would later lend itself to the 'midday demon'. In French, *une méridienne* is a piece of furniture, a day-bed designed for siestas, which was very fashionable during the First Empire, at the beginning of the nineteenth century. Because 'midday' is a delicate moment, dangerous to traverse, this 'unique hour' is associated with ghosts by Servius and with superstition by Plutarch. No serious undertaking is suited to this moment of the day. Midday marks the highest point in the sun's diurnal course; which explains why so many of the rites related to solar worship are performed at this time, and why, for other religions, the hour is considered ill-omened. Islam warns the Muslim not to pray to the Prophet at this unholy hour, which is reserved only for sun worshippers... According to the Aztecs, 'midday' is the most propitious time for sacrifice while, for many Indo-European races, it is the hour of the dead, if not death itself... In Greek mythology, the Nymphs appear at 'midday' to try and catch Pan up in their dance. Roger Caillois notes: 'Such is the nature of nympholepsy: whoever is exposed to the influence of the Nymphs, those "goddesses who never sleep, feared by the inhabitants of the fields", is seized by a sacred or prophetic frenzy.' Later he states that the Nymphs cast their spells at this fateful hour, and that madness then takes a hold. Midday is a terrible hour. Taking their siesta in the shade of their homes, city dwellers are clearly sheltered from both the sun's touch and that of madness, but what about the shepherds, the herdsmen? Furthermore, Pan masturbates habitually, inciting the shepherds to give themselves up to the practice. How can you refuse such an invitation, coming as it does from a god, when you are a lonely shepherd, weighed down by the heat, half asleep, dreaming of impossible loves, longing for unbridled couplings? In her entry for 'Pan' in the *Dictionnaire des mythologies*[4], Stella Georgoudi supplies some important information: 'Pan's direct influence upon the sex life of the group takes a much firmer hold when the latter responds sympathetically to the characteristically prodigious sexual activities of the god himself. Pan is an ithyphallic deity, a seducer (*lagnos*), given to love (*erôtikos*), lewd as a rutting donkey (*kêlon*), overflowing with seed (*polusporos*): a pursuer of Nymphs, whose cries resound through the caves during their secret unions with the god (*Panos gamoi*: Euripides, *Helen*, 190). He also chases the young shepherds (Pan, the 'pederast') and when he is without a partner, seeks satisfaction from his own self. Masturbation, which Pan taught to the shepherds, according to Diogenes the Cynic (Dio Chrysostom, 6, 203 f R), is a particular characteristic of goatherds, whose general lasciviousness became a byword in marked contrast to the self-control of the cowherds. (Theocritus, *Idylls*, I,86a).' Don't forget that Pan is not just the result of a union between Penelope and Hermes, but a Hermes transformed into a goat, which he considered to be an animal 'inclined towards pleasures': hence his fondness for goatherds. Similarly, 'midday' is a time of high sexual intensity, through which daily torrents of sperm flow... How many dozing shepherds did the Sirens bestride? How many secret and joyful couplings between peasant and succubus were achieved amid these rustic meadows? How many erotic dreams have resulted from those moments during a siesta when sexual desire is accompanied by a liberating, automatic gesture which takes place half-consciously or, as one might say, in a half-tint? Whatever the answer may be, there are numerous mythological accounts which associate 'midday' with supernatural fecundity, the inseminating of 'virgin mothers', the derangement of the senses and the loosening of conventions. Is this fragment of sleep, this panning from the night into day, always carnal? It's clear that a siesta of 'easy virtue' has troubled more than one woman, more than one man. This exquisite moment is mixed at times with fear, provoking panic: a word directly derived, in case you ever doubted it, from 'Pan'.

The 'midday demon' was the subject of a novel by Paul Bourget (*The Midday Demon*) first published in 1914 and has also tortured several poets, such as Leconte de Lisle, whose 'Midday' can be found in his collection *Antique Poems*, which in turn influenced

José-Maria de Heredia while he was writing 'The Siesta', published in *Trophies*.

Not a single sound of insect or crawling bee;
All is sleeping beneath great boughs, weighed down
by the sun,
Whose dense foliage sifts the light of such a day
Upon the dark velvet softness of this emerald moss

Piercing the dark dome, Midday prowls in splendour,
While upon my half-closed eyelids, languid with sleep,
A thousand stealthy flashes form a scarlet network
Which, interlaced, stretches out across the burning
shadows.

Towards the veil of flames woven by the light
Flies a fragile swarm of richly coloured butterflies,
Grown drunk upon the light and the scent of nectar

It's then that my trembling fingers seize each thread
And, in golden nets of this subtle fibre,
A peaceful hunter, I entrap my dreams.

The Disciplinary Timetable

A siesta can vary in length from a handful of minutes to several hours. It is not some kind of *hapax legomenon*, but a word designating something which traverses both time and nation. 'But what are you talking about?' 'The Siesta!' 'Siesta?' Quick, my *Dictionnaire historique de la langue française*[5]: 'Siesta, feminine noun, first introduced (1681) from the Spanish *siesta*, derived from the Latin *sexta (hora)*, "the sixth hour", i.e. "the middle of the day" or "midday", the Romans dividing the day, from sunrise to sunset, into twelve equal "hours" whose length varied according to the season.' A more recent lexicon states that the verb 'to siesta' ('*siester*', 1872), meaning 'to take a siesta', is 'a current part of African French' implying that its use, along with the words '*siesteur*' and '*siesteuse*', is extremely rare within France's own hexagonal borders. According to Jean Chevalier and Alain Gheerbrant in their *Dictionnaire des symboles*[6], the number six is associated in *The Book of Revelation* with sin. It is Nero's number – the sixth Emperor. It is also the Creator's number. God, you will recall, created Heaven and Earth, the animals and plants, man and woman etc. in six extraordinarily crowded days.

Returning to the hexagon, its six sides represent for the Hindus 'the penetration of the yoni by the lingam, the balancing of water by fire and the symbol of outward expansion (*rajas*) which constitutes manifestation'. The six-pointed Star of David is also an expression of the macrocosm. As for the Mayans, the sixth day was taboo, bringing death while, to the Bambara, it marks the opportunity to bear male twins (3+3)... As with most magic and symbolic numbers, six is ambivalent. The sixth hour, that is to say 'midday', calls the early Christians to prayer, just as it chimes with the afternoon, calling for a siesta. In fact, right up to the start of the seventeenth century, the morning meal in the West was eaten around 10am, it being understood that midday would immediately follow! Throughout the seventeenth and eighteenth centuries, lunch was served between eleven and noon, and only among urban populations in the second half of the nineteenth century was it taken between noon and one, setting the siesta back by an hour.

As for '*sext*' (12pm), it is a prayer belonging to the canonical day, along with '*prime*' (6am), '*terce* ' (9am) and '*nones*' (3pm). Tertullian counted these last three as moments for daily meditation: 'It was at *terce* that the Holy Spirit descended upon the gathered Apostles; at *sext*, Saint Peter, on the day he had the vision of the vessel filled with all manner of meats, climbed up on the housetop to pray; at *nones* he went with John to the Temple where he cured the lame man of his paralysis.' The liturgical day, according to *Genesis*, begins in the evening. 'And God called the light Day, and the darkness he called Night, and the evening and morning were the first day' (*Genesis* I.5) *Matins* is rung at midnight, followed by *laudes* at 3am. *Prime*, at 6am announces Mass and the start of the day, which is divided from sunrise to sunset into twelve hours, more or less identical to each other, from one country to another and from one season to another. *Prime*, *terce*, *sext*, *nones* and *vespers* apply to every kind of populace from the fields to the cities, while *matins*, *laudes* and *compline* more particularly concern the monastic world. In the sixth century, the order of Saint Benedict prescribed a siesta after lunch for its members, especially from Easter to October, taking great pains over the repose of its Benedictines, who could sleep between six and eight hours at a time. Despite being strictly regulated, monastic life allowed for small morsels of time to be plucked up, as one fingers the beads on a rosary.

According to Lewis Mumford, American historian of technology, the key machine of the modern Industrial era isn't the steam engine; it's the clock[7], one that ascribes a new chronology to capitalism. Between the thirteenth and fifteenth centuries, in all the major cities throughout Christendom, the water clock or *clepsydra* (a Latin borrowing from the Greek *'klepsudra'*, meaning 'water thief') was replaced by the mechanical timepiece. Not only was it equipped with a face and hands, it also possessed a bell with which to sound all the hours of the day. The regularity with which time now passed would progressively impose a discipline upon human rhythm and regulate the hours of work. It was probably around 1345 that the division of the hour into sixty minutes, and the minute into sixty seconds, spread throughout the city's ruling classes, transforming each individual's time – previously regulated by the rhythms of the heart, of the breath and other activities – into a homogeneous, abstract time: the reference point of one time for all. When one considers the day as the passage of abstract time, a utility, Lewis Mumford has observed[8], one is not going to turn in with the chickens on winter nights. One invents candles, chimneys, gaslight, electric bulbs in order to fill all the hours of the day. When people think of time not as a succession of experiences but as a collection of hours, minutes and seconds, they acquire the habit of increasing it or hoarding it. Freeing himself from the 'natural' cycles of day and night, the seasons and the stages of life, the citizen submits himself to constricted time, determined by the inflexible automaton. Over several centuries, and not without setbacks, the timepiece, which once disported itself on high in a steeple or belfry, shrank down to the domestic clock and then into the individual watch. Acquiring a watch did not only involve adorning oneself with a sign of social rank, but also hoarding it and, if necessary, using it as security and hocking it. If the first watches were available only to the moneyed classes, the watch was by the end of the eighteenth century 'democratic' enough in Industrial Europe for the British Prime Minister William Pitt to impose a tax on its ownership. This was a widely unpopular decision provoking anger and occasional humour as in this song suggested by the *Morning Chronicle* for December 18, 1797:

> If your Money he take – why your Breeches remain;
> And the flaps of your Shirts, if your Breeches he gain;
> And your skin, if your Shirts; and if shoes, your bare feet.
> Then never mind TAXES – *We've beat the Dutch fleet!*

The Prime Minister proposed some amendments, such as one intending only to start imposing the tax upon households with two watches or more... This measure only lasted a few months. It certainly didn't prevent the watch from establishing itself as an indispensable possession, or the poor from being obliged to acquire one: on credit if needs be, thanks to the Clock and Watch Clubs. Furthermore, anything so capable of selling itself could just as easily be resold or pawned, as historian E.P. Thompson reveals in this anecdotal account[9]: 'This 'ere ticker,' said a London typesetter from the 1820s, 'cost me but a five-pun note ven I bort it fust, and I've popped it more than twenty times, and had more than forty poun' on it altogether. It's a gajian haingel to a feller, is a good votch, ven you're hard up.' But a 'watch' only has value so long as mechanical time, machine time – that is to say, modern time – completely organizes social existence and imposes itself upon the individual. The discipline of the industrial process has escaped the confines of the factory floor and dictates more and more of our timetable. Goodbye to the unforeseen, the unscheduled – the surprise. Henceforth, 'time waits for no man' would resound like an order outside this inflexible regime and not as a greeting! Except that children can still (but for how much longer?) take the scholastic route...and play truant.

The mediaevalist Jacques Le Goff[10] explains how the Church, having established liturgical time throughout every form of mediaeval society by the rhythmic sounding of its bells (the church tower being an invention of the sixth and seventh centuries), was forced to compete, from the end of the thirteenth century onwards, with 'commercial time', secular time, wage-earner time: urban time *par excellence*. Le Goff stresses one insufficiently studied fact: the remarkable slide of the hour ascribed to *nones*, the time for rest and dining in the High Middle Ages which had originally occurred around two o'clock in the afternoon, towards midday. In the urban workplace of the fourteenth century a new physical unit of time was introduced: the half-day. Let us not forget, however, that these changes in the passage of time – this regulatory chopping, this conflict between liturgical time and that of commerce, travel and manual production – complement more than they oppose each other. Reality is incredibly complex, mutable and plural: not just at the level of continents, where the days don't correspond with each other, but also at the regional level and even that of city districts. It is still possible in our age (but with increasing rarity, it must be said) to hear the bells of the Christian church, the muezzin's call to prayer from the summit of a mosque's minaret or the fire station's siren on the first Wednesday of every month: all expressions of the different timescales, religious or otherwise, which can inhabit the same space.

Mumford, Le Goff and Thompson, to cite only three historians, take great pains to emphasize the heterogeneous nature of the processes involved in the rational organization of productive time – through industrialization and waged work – that took place at the heart of society. Rural areas were also affected by the secular time of merchants and manufacturers which brought an end to the 'putting out system' of working at home. Everyone inhabited several times at once: city time, work time (in the factories as well as the fields), religious observance and belief time and communal time (based around the family, the village, the neighbourhood). 'We are entering here already in 1700', E.P. Thompson observes[11] 'the familiar landscape of disciplined industrial capitalism, with the time-sheet, the time-keeper, the informers and fines.' 'Informer' clocks already exist to expose indolent or tardy workers. Regimentation in the countryside will be more sensitive but just as unyielding. In fact, agricultural workers – the 'journeymen', or day-labourers, whose title is linked to the amount of land that can be worked in a single day – are scattered across the fields, where their activities are less easy to gauge against the clock, which makes controlling them difficult. The adoption of stricter timetables and the establishing of standards for productivity and profits will be made easier by the mechanization of farm work. The wandering countryman, given to siestas and dreams but also ready to work, will no longer be able to organize his daily activities according to his mood. He will have to obey an externally imposed regime, completely foreign to his way of life. Work in the fields has for a long time evaded the ticking of the clock, permitting country dwellers to harmonize their time with that of nature... Without accepting all of Jean Giono's critique of technology in his remarkable novel, *The Weight of Heaven*[12], I can't help passing on the following proposal, even if some of his words require closer definition: 'The natural function of life is to live. To live is to seek joy in nature. Joy is not a product of society or technology. It is the individual product that an individual being, rich in natural treasures, is better qualified than anyone else to attain and to keep, so long as his physical being inhabits the space and time of a man. Mankind lives among unbounded splendours.' The siesta is certainly one of these 'unbounded splendours'; it is part of what defines these 'splendours', one of its freedoms, one of its possibilities. This break in the straight path of waged employment indicates a surprise, a detour, a sidetrack. The siesta is a sidetrack leading away from all activity that is distinct, obligatory, habitual and mechanical. The originality of the work that each of us hopes to achieve depends largely upon our retaining control of our own time. When it comes to the hours spent on waged work, you must inevitably render an account of their content. Your employer aims to make you as productive as possible and to avoid downtime. The organizational skills of Frederick W. Taylor are well known: how he cut out mishaps and lapses which were, to his way of thinking, opportunities for idleness... Meanwhile employees rack their brains over how to snatch back, here and there, any scrap of the time they have bartered, sold short or lost in jobs which aren't always worthwhile. Ever since the first appearance of rules dividing up workers' activities according to precise timetables, strikes and wage demands have been defined in terms of 'working hours'. The amount of sociological texts and eyewitness accounts concerning piece-work and, more generally, Taylor's 'Principles of Scientific Management' and their subsequent refinements, is enormous and can be summed up in one image – symbolic in so many ways – taken from the poster for Charlie Chaplin's *Modern Times*: a worker transformed into a cog, inside a machine made up of cogs to which he is entirely subordinate. The arrangement of gears suggests the inner workings of a watch. Industrial time feeds upon the individual time of every man and woman who clocks on at a factory. Numerous revolts have taken place against this imposed time, from one of the first 'modern' strikes in fourteenth-century Florence through to our own day, via disputes in mediaeval cloth-manufacturing cities over the *Werkglocken*, or work-bells, which kept a loose tally of workers' attendance... The aftermath of May '68 is characterized by films, novels and slogans attacking the notion of time confiscated solely for the benefit of economic rationalization and by communal efforts to establish alternative ways of working to support alternative ways of occupying one's time. The culture of the working day, however, has so completely pervaded our way of life that it seems absurd to pretend that one can detach oneself from it by means of the siesta. The many proposals for readjusting work-time, and for its reduction, have continued to provoke stiff resistance from politicians, CEOs and even certain trade unionists and wage-earners. Even though in this age of 'new technology', the capitalist system of production is redefining waged work, trying to replace it with 'flexitime' (that is to say, by making it conform to the rhythms of both production and consumption – service industry timetables have increasingly broken free from the regimentation of the 'Fordist' era in order to meet the new demands of 'consumers' who no longer share the same timetable so that stores now stay open late during the week and on Sundays too), the realignment of constricted time with personal time not only remains unsystematic but unimaginable as well. Once again theory lags behind (the siesta!), thanks to the accelerated change in work taking place throughout most of the post-industrial nations. André Gorz has made a remarkable study of this change in his study *Today's Poverty, Tomorrow's Riches*[13]. He reveals that the question is not so much one of a work 'crisis' (something which is almost without meaning since work is both fundamental to our being and, when understood in terms of 'making' or 'doing', incapable of disappearing) but of a profound and clearly irreversible transformation taking place within the wage-earning classes. It is work in the form of permanent, full-time, salaried employment that is threatened by changes in conditions for the production of wealth. The fact is that 'capital', as a factor of production, no longer invests itself or makes a profit for itself as it once did in the triumphant days of industrial capitalism. It is also a fact that 'work', considered as a factor of production, can no longer fulfil the same function within so radically transformed a context. The effects – and the dangers – of the 'new technology' stem from how the thinking behind the old liberal political economy has overflowed it, slipping away to slide, like a wave on a sandy beach, over the cultural, the irregular and the vernacular. In other words, an economy linked to the use of information and communication technologies can no longer be understood in terms of the economic sciences (?!) but finds certain elements of its explanation in the 'non-economic'. Here André Gorz is catching up with Ivan Illich who for years had been running himself ragged trying to popularize the concept of 'disvalue'. By this term he sought to designate that which evades economic calculation yet is still essential to life. If Illich makes use of a word unknown to the dictionaries, it is not only to fill a need but also to break with a way of thinking. In fact, he writes: 'By coining the concept of disvalue both the homologies and the contradictions that exist between social and physical degradation can be shown. While physical 'work' tends to increase entropy, the economic productivity of work is based on the previous dis-valuation of cultural labour. Waste and degradation are usually considered as side effects in the production of values. I suggest precisely the opposite. I argue that economic value accumulates only as a result of the previous wasting of culture, which can also be considered as the creation of disvalue.'[14] In order to liberate us from economic logic, together with the arrogant discourse of its acolytes (which attempts to explain the proliferation of new technology throughout every society on the planet), Illich takes great care to accompany his thoughts on 'disvalue' with an analysis of 'commons' and 'blessings'. He observes: 'People called "commons" that part of the environment for which customary law exacted specific forms of community respect.' An example of commons in our own time? Silence. Yes, indeed. Silence can be taken from us by machines capable of imitating it and improving upon its appearance, of killing true silence with its false substitute, just as a machine can take the voice of its owner, record it, broadcast it and copy it, or a machine can remember what we do not wish to forget... I would also suggest a further example: the siesta. Here is a small piece of behavioural knowledge – insignificant, banal, everyday and ordinary – which is in danger of becoming institutionalized, prescribed, redeemed, medicalized, taxed, taught and professionalized. And as for 'blessings', they belong to the cultural order but are obscured by an economic system which devalues them in order to be rid of them. As an example, Illich cites a Japanese family who, having sent their grandmother off to a 'medicalized' institution, loses forever a number of blessings ranging 'from the height of laughter to the sad bitterness of tears'. I would similarly offer, instead of the siesta itself (which is a disvalue), the well-being that it permits, the rest it procures and the dreams that it welcomes like a surprise gift. A time spent doing nothing? It is, however, a blessed 'nothing'. Such a time possesses a 'value' without price, as in Jean Duvignaud's definition of art. The siesta is a means for us to reclaim our own time, outside the clockmakers' control. The siesta is our liberator.

IV

A Time to Oneself

My maternal grandfather used to be quite vigorous about his siestas. There was, however, nothing of the hermit or the monk about him. He would organize his time by savouring it, by measuring – perhaps better than we can today – its breadth. He was not the only one. A reading of André Gide's *Journal*, or Thomas Mann's, is enough to confirm for us the importance of the siesta to those born in the nineteenth century. This also seems to be true for many of the characters inhabiting the fiction of Jorge Amado, Yachar Kemal, Tewfik El Hakim, Miguel Angel Asturias and Rabindranath Tagore; the siesta is a defining moment for meditation, reflection, dreams, enjoyment or sleep. Beneficent siesta: repose which is conducive to relaxation. It is often justified by climactic considerations: the midday heat enforces inaction, pushing men into the café to play dominoes while sipping tea and puffing on a hookah, or to lie down in the shade of a cheese tree or in the cool confines of a room with drawn blinds. It has more to do, however, with an almost universal art of living – no matter how violent the sun may be. In the depths of winter Tolstoy happily gave himself to the ritual of the siesta – one shared with those societies where the political economy and its rationalization ('time is money!') has yet to infiltrate every crevice of daily life. It would be tedious for the reader to compile a list, albeit one that is far from exhaustive, of every author who has invoked, at whatever length, the siesta. When you begin to mark in the margins of a novel, journal or collection of letters the number of times that the word 'siesta' appears, you can only be astonished at its frequency. How many principal characters, male and female, doze off for a few seconds after lunch? How many novelists organize their day's writing around that key reference point: the siesta? The watchword here: don't put off until tomorrow the siesta you can take today.

The siesta's long history, together with its presence in the many societies still not completely modernized, would foster the belief that it describes a practice destined to disappear along with the last traces of rural tradition. The siesta, however, is just as much an urban affair; and, in a world that is fast becoming increasingly urbanized, one has the right to claim for oneself the time that it would once have taken up. A wider question presents itself here. How, and into what forms, has the urbanization of behaviour transformed the rhythms of daily life? Today's citizen inhabits several temporalities at once: those of local government and public services with their hours of availability; businesses and their schedules; schools with their weekly timetable and calendar of vacations; those determined by the changes in the environment, built or otherwise; and those of individual private existence with its expectations, hopes, illusions, 'times out', etc. The modern city, born of industrialization and mechanized transport, is an endless vortex, constantly renewing connections, exchanges and encounters. Baudelaire was intoxicated – and wearied – by the city's uninterrupted flow of people and things. The modern city is a complex machine, wary of dead time. It is upon time, rather than space, that the city has most left its mark: in regularity, punctuality, planned flexibility, repetition, periodicity etc. Everyday time has been shaped by the demands of the city's multiple activities. In a similar manner, the train has slowly imposed its timetable upon all those activities related to transportation and 'circulation'. The station clock attracts everyone's eye, serving as a meeting-point. The necessary harmonization both of time between cities in the same country (with Paris time becoming the national time in 1891) and of that between railway stations in different countries, in order to facilitate connections and regulate the movement of men and machines, led the various nation states to provide themselves with a standardized timescale. Not without difficulty and much equivocation did the railroad companies of Europe and America adopt Greenwich Mean Time in 1882 as a common reference point and to make their timetables commensurable with one another. Summoned into a state of permanence by different temporalities, city-dwellers have lost control of their own true biological time. They accept (just how does one oppose it?) the regulation of their time by the rhythms of 'the city' and, more specifically, by those of its economy: financial transactions, markets, businesses and production lines. The most striking example of economic time's victory over the biological time of every living human being is the system's '3/8' time-signature. The steel mill, the blast furnace and the assembly line are all sustained by this 'primal rhythm'. The enormous accumulation of literature, from the 1930s onwards, dedicated to these rhythms – and I'm thinking here of medical research into the rhythms of both the human body and each of its individual organs, sexual and reproductive rhythms, including those of sleep and chronobiology – ignored the diversity of urban time. In his study, *In Search of Time and Rhythm*[15], for example, André Missenard worries over the 'probable emergence of a species of citizen different from the natural model' under the influence of 'excess stimulation, coupled with the constant exciting of the senses by the hectic life of the new city'. It's a universal axiom that the modern city is a place of velocities, crowded boulevards, unexpected changes and an overexertion of the senses, leading to a jangling of the 'nerves' and giving rise to 'anxieties': what the American doctor George M. Beard, in his 1881 study *American Nervousness*, termed 'neurasthenia'. The pressures that urban living exerts upon every single one of us communicate themselves in their various forms as 'stress'. This English word, designating 'overwork', is derived from the old French, '*destrece*', meaning 'distress'. The siesta is an excellent antidote to this anonymous, but nonetheless destructive, assault upon our physical and mental well-being. Gustave Thibon in 'The Rhythms of Spiritual Life'[16], having sadly observed how little interest the subject holds for philosophers, explains his notion of rhythm: 'It is important at this point not to confuse rhythm, which is a living phenomenon, with its mechanical imitations...mechanical alternation restates the identical, while live alternation reaffirms the similar. Measure repeats; rhythm renews. Natural cycles always allow for the unforeseeable. This margin for the unexpected expands to embrace higher orders of phenomena. One can calculate the precise movement of the stars, while biological, psychological and historical cycles are never completely symmetrical but contain within each of their alternations something irreducibly new.' Sleep during the night and the day – including the siesta – breaks with just such regularity and depends upon factors that are not always identifiable.

Gustave Thibon is, however, a little hard on philosophy. As it happens, certain philosophers from before the Second World War, such as Jean-Marie Guyau, then Henri Bergson, Gaston Bachelard and Vladimir Jankélévitch, became interested in rhythm via questions of 'time' and 'duration'. Georg Simmel was, in fact, concerned with urban rhythms in his study of the individual within the big city[17]. To this end he describes 'the intensification of the nervous existence' of the city-dweller, explaining that 'the big city creates exactly the right psychological conditions at every street corner, through the rhythm and diversity of life, whether social, professional and economic. Through the degree of awareness which it demands from us in order to organize ourselves as separate entities, it establishes from the first tender foundations of life and the spirit, a profound antipathy towards small-town and rural existence, where the life of the senses is structured to a slower, more habitual rhythm and flows regularly.' Is he thinking here of the siesta, which is a common practice in villages but has become less distinct in the city? In more philosophical, less anthropological terms, Gaston Bachelard's essay 'The Intuition of the Moment'[18], commenting upon the work of his friend Gaston Roupnel, finishes up by favouring the moment over duration and the accidental over the repetitive, the continuous and the mensural. Duration, for him, is irremediably heterogeneous: 'a dusting of moments', as he so beautifully puts it. According to my reading of Bachelard, the siesta is an eternally singular moment that shapes daily existence: a habit, in the sense of 'an act restored through its newness'. Time, understood as the unfinished, yet perpetually recommenced creation of our 'being', perpetuates itself both in and through change, with the accident of the moment: unexpected, yet part of the present. Inspired by Lucio Alberto Pinheiro dos Santos' memoir *Rhythmanalysis*[19], Gaston Bachelard devised a rhythmanalytical method to grasp more fully the chronologically infinite possibilities of human existence. Human life is a succession of experiences whose order is not always apparent. In *The Dialectics of Duration*[20], he observes: 'In renewing a form, rhythm often restores a materiality, an energy. Matter is not arranged in space, indifferent to time; nor does it exist as a constant, completely inert for a changeless duration. It *exists*, within the full meaning of the term, on the level of rhythm.' Such an *existence* inscribes itself through a dialectics of tension and relaxation, of alternation between periods of busyness and calm, motion and rest. According to Bachelard, rest can be 'busy' and activity 'passive', but each 'instance' is unique and its repetition illusory since, by necessity, it must mark the conclusion of something. What remains, but not always in a perceptible form, is that which has been handed down to us from our childhood. It lies hidden, revealing itself without warning. It is because our 'being' is a mystery which fortunately illuminates itself every so often in our understanding that the study of rhythms constitutes a method of analysis, or even self-analysis. In *Lautréamont*[21], Bachelard explains: 'More systematic than Psychoanalysis, Rhythmanalysis seeks out the patterns of duality in spiritual activity. It rediscovers the distinction between unconscious tendencies and the efforts of consciousness; but it balances more effectively than Psychoanalysis the tendencies towards opposing poles: the double motion of psychism.' The imagination can decode this paradox: a motion pretending to be its opposite, a fixed point moving by itself. This is what he discovered in Mallarmé's poetry[22]. 'It is not his message that everything that grows must spring forth, even the lilacs of April. When one reflects that Mallarmé's spring is primarily a nostalgic yearning for the lucidity of winter, one feels inclined to imagine that this growth is subterranean, that it shares its life with that of the root. The time has not yet come to arise. It is still necessary *to wait*: to wait inside the abyss or, better yet, while being swallowed up by the abyss.' Like the seasons in Mallarmé's poetry, the rhythms that condition our 'being' are both multiple and varied. Commenting on the work of Pinheiro dos Santos in *The Dialectics of Duration*, Bachelard notes that: 'It is the lack of an active sublimation – attractive, emergent, positively creative – that upsets the balance of psychoanalytic ambiguity and disturbs the play of psychic values. To be incapable of *actualizing* an ideal love is clearly a misfortune. To be incapable of *idealizing* an actual love is yet another.' Here one rediscovers the extraordinary curiosity and patience of a philosopher who refuses to erase anything that might be written down during a lifetime. Everything must be kept. Everything makes sense, even nonsense. Everything changes, even stability. 'For the individual,' he declares, 'evolution is woven out of successes and mistakes.' What is so formidable about Bachelard is the force – and the evidence – of his formulations. Listen to this: 'It is within the impersonal part of the individual that the philosopher must discover the zones of repose, and the reasons for repose, from which he will create a philosophical system for repose.' Or even this: 'The furrow is the temporal axis of work, while the evening's repose marks the boundary of the field.' For Bachelard, it is understood that 'repose is a happy vibration': precisely the same one that I feel during a siesta. The well-earned rest, the stop which prepares for the next departure, this pause which seeks to be a presence in itself: that is to say, an absence of others so that one might be more amenable towards them afterwards. The siesta? An uncertain 'afterwards' connected to a demonstrable 'before'. That which Bachelard calls an 'event', others would call a 'moment' in the sense of 'there isn't a moment to lose, to lose oneself and to be reborn, to become new'. During the 1970s and 1980s, Henri Lefebvre, sociologist of the everyday, renewed an acquaintance with Bachelard's approach, recommending in his own way an examination of temporalities: the thousand and one threads from which the individual weaves an existence. His *Elements of Rhythmanalysis*[23] describes itself as an 'introduction to the understanding of rhythm', proposing to augment the triad of 'time-space-energy' with that of 'melody-harmony-rhythm' through an awareness that 'everywhere there's an interaction of place, time and a release of energy, there is also a rhythm'. His search for rhythms, and for what their intelligibility conveys to us, is presented as something more than a simple phenomenological approach, a surpassing of appearances, or a will to seize the present time of a thing or condition in order to transform it into a presence. Such an emphasis on presence contains unmistakably existential undertones, which Lefebvre seeks to both energize and poeticize. Modern life never ceases to disjoint, separate, divide, fragment and erode; and it does so to human beings just as much as to the actions they perform and the goods they use, whatever work, space, time or multiple occupations it might contain. The 'everyday' comprises the totality of daily facts and daily gestures. What's important here is *totality*: that is to say, the linkage involved, together with the arguments that lie behind it, however voluntary or ordained they may be. This linkage is sometimes experienced as being heavy and coercive: a literal chaining together. Sociologists, either following on from the pioneering work of Henri Lefebvre or in the wake of Joffre Dumazedier and his studies on leisure, have laid out everyday time for examination, classifying it according to age, sex, 'socio-professional grouping' etc., and can, as a result, establish comparative profiles. They can also distribute each individual 'time allocation' between several 'uses' (transport, training, consumption, leisure and work, for example). The Greeks had already marked out the 'bio-periodic processes', but it was scholars from France (J.J. Virey and his study of chronopharmacology in 1814) and Germany (E. Bünning and his work on vegetable rhythms) who first introduced the analysis of biological rhythms. All living beings (both flora and fauna) share with 'humans' the principle of being temporally organized. Biological rhythms are genetic in origin but depend equally upon a large number of factors, both 'internal' and 'external'. 'In the human organism,' Alain Reinberg observes[24], 'temperature, arterial pressure, the sleep/waking cycle, metabolized substances, hormones, enzymes, tiredness, alertness, memory, along with over 180 other processes, change according to biological rhythms that occur within a period of approximately 24 hours in most cases (circadian rhythms being derived from the Latin *circa*, 'approximately' and *diem* 'day') and one year in others.' It goes without saying that no one biological rhythm is regulated by any other. Diversity is of the essence. This is confirmed by the researches of Paul Fraisse in the field of chronopsychology, which seek to understand the connections between chronobiology and the specific rhythms of intellectual and cognitive activity. Such a discovery, however, will not make life any easier for anyone timetabling group activities! For several years now, the pharmaceutical companies have vied with each other in ingenuity over the problem of intellectual rhythms as much as they have over the chronotherapeutic and chronokinetic properties of certain drugs. All the same, the siesta has yet to become the subject of any special experiments. A scientific inquiry into the rhythms of the 'everyday' must be linked to literature and to cinema, both of which have fastened themselves, sometimes skilfully, upon the tiniest daily activities, revealing to what extent the banal, the repetitive and the 'low-grade' conceal treasures, joys and 'small' blessings. Thus, mixed in with the linear time marked out by the wristwatch are the unequal – and not necessarily synchronous – daily temporalities of every individual in step with different social times. It's entirely appropriate to observe and to appreciate such complex and undisciplined dialectical play. In this context, the siesta appears as truly free time, belonging to no-one but the person who takes it. It is a moment, no matter how long or how short, where one is *placed in the presence of oneself* through a momentary absence from the world. This ephemeral retreat offers a shelter for the reunion, reunification and temporary reconstitution of our shattered, divided and scattered selves. This pause, by virtue of the rest it both supplies and guarantees to us all, helps to restore our integrity. This brief interval allows us to take our bearings, just as the sailor marks his position and plots his course while all around him the elements either rage or subside. The siesta functions as a metaphor here, acquiring another meaning: one that no longer only refers to the act of falling asleep or dozing in the middle of the day, but also to the capacity we have to dictate the use of our own time rather than selling it short by submitting ourselves to time imposed by 'society'. Increasingly, city-dwellers no longer work near their homes and cannot return there for a rest at siesta time, which is why those taking siestas tend not to be actively involved in full-time employment but are usually students, freelance travellers (ranging from the commercial to the more liberal professions), instructors, researchers, artists or retired people: those who have, for good or ill, achieved control over their daily schedules. This 'privilege' is worth any raise in salary, providing as it does so many of the conditions for both physical and mental well-being.

The siesta is not best liked by either the human or the social sciences. Neither are anthropologists nor sociologists interested in the subject. Don't believe me? Scour the classics in these fields and you won't find one entry for 'siesta' in their indexes: not in Émile Durkheim, Marcel Mauss or Malinowski, nor in Evans-Pritchard, Lévi-Strauss or Margaret Mead. Yet the communities they studied took siestas on a more or less ritualistic basis. One thing is certain: the siesta played a part in the temporal organization of those societies considered 'without history'. Doesn't it deserve a mention in the same chapters as those on 'body attitudes' or 'daily life', or in the understanding of 'classification by age' or in examinations of 'gender differences', and under its own heading as do 'silence', 'waiting', 'inaction' and the 'dream'? What place does the siesta occupy in human life, not only for the individual but also in the deep tissue of social relationships and collective arrangements? As we have seen with the 'midday demon', this 'in between' hour was presented in myths as a bringer of sensuality and suggestive of certain attitudes. And yet mythologists, even those familiar with the workings of the imagination, do not treat the siesta with the respect it deserves. A few sociologists and psychologists have studied how everyday time is divided up according to social class (such as the working class), or a specific age group (such as fifteen to twenty year-olds or 'students') without ever once confronting the siesta directly. The same goes for historians, who have narrated for us the story of the bed, the sheet, the bolster, the pillowcase, snoring, sleepwalking and insomnia but never the siesta. Wouldn't it be useful, however, to sample the feelings that sleep aroused in our ancestors? And their dreaming too? How did they sleep? And what did they dream? What was their attitude towards the siesta? What relationships did they establish between rest and action, between the act of repose and physical health? What a raft of subjects for a thesis!

It's just the same with geographers, who have charted forests, deserts, coastlines and proposed geographies of honey and rice, honour, crime and poverty, holocausts, obesity and who knows what else. There is no geography of the siesta, however, let alone a comparative geopolitical study!

The same applies to economists: not one calculation has been carried out to gauge its effects at a macro-economic level, or to figure out the losses and gains of this time which, although spent outside work and the economy, feeds back upon both the work and economy of society as a whole. Raising these questions with friends who are 'reputable' economists – and who also managed politely not to smile at my request – I was met with only an embarrassed silence. To make my proposal sound more serious I (rather maliciously) mentioned the non-existence of statistics on the 'economic cost of Ramadan', Paul Balta's essay in *The State of Religions* notwithstanding... Having observed it at first hand, I am persuaded that a siesta, however brief, restores a certain edge – which is something that I am careful not to shout from the rooftops. Imagine an astute employer – some do exist – who allows you to set your own timetable and says to you 'don't forget to take a little siesta, my friend: it will help you relax' in the knowledge that it will make you more productive. Beware of such manipulation! Beware of this vicious appropriation! This perverse alienation! What's this? He's giving me back my siesta? Keeping an analytical tally of such exploitation, this honest man demonstrates to his peers the accuracy of his calculations, justifies it, goes from one international seminar to another, presents before parliament the outline for a bill on 'siesta-vouchers'... in short, his campaigning on behalf of the siesta doesn't make him any less your boss. Careful attention should be paid to the thought that an illegal siesta exerts a superior charm to that of a compulsory one...the charm of the forbidden. Urbanization, together with the new geography it creates, often renders the siesta impossible. However, there are certain pockets of resistance, surrounded like the villages in *Asterix* by the modern world and its cohorts of new constraints, which have not yet surrendered. In Spain and Italy, for example, siesta-time is a true cultural blessing, even if that time is used for doing other things. In China, according to Bruno Comby[25], 'the siesta is called *xiu-xi*, and the right to a siesta is guaranteed by Article 49 of the 1949 Constitution.' In his survey on 'The Art of the Siesta'[26], Francis Mizio denounced French tardiness in this matter: there is still, despite Corsica, an appreciable national deficit in siestas. Nevertheless, he informs us, that 'a French company, CAE Communications, is the first to offer the world the possibility of a cyber-siesta via the Internet (www.cae.fr/espfun/sieste:sieste.htm) offering images of the countryside accompanied by soothing ambient sounds dedicated to dozing off in front of the computer.' If Northern Europe hides itself away for its siesta, Latin America makes a show of the pleasure to be found in the taking of one, as do both Africa and Asia, down to the smallest degree. The turmoil of the big cities, the adoption of international timetables, the prevalence of air-conditioning, plus the ideological supremacy of work and money, have relegated the siesta to those practices that are ancestral, rustic, traditional and unproductive. To defend the siesta within such a context is to go up against political correctness in this matter. Citizens are becoming increasingly worried about their unavailability ('I no longer have a minute to myself!'), their over-consumption of time, their longing both to use it more economically and to ease up. In 1977, New York MD Stephan Rechtschaffen founded the Omega Institute, which took in 'time-sick' people and taught them to (once again) savour time. In 1990, Peter Heintel, Professor of Philosophy at the University of Klagenfurt in Austria, founded the Tempus group to mobilize those who are skilled in taking their time. Much more preferable to fast food are the 'slow food' restaurants to be found in Berlin, for example. The breakneck pace of the subway system can be countered by standing still on the moving walkways or escalators, adopting the drifter's stroll, the random stop, the imaginary halt, the pause for breath, the rest. Confronted by a high-speed world, from the parking meter to the pizza delivery service, it is both desirable and possible to slow oneself down, to discover one's *well-being in patience*, to savour each moment as a hymn to duration, a homage to life. This new understanding of time, this extended complicity with each minute, this true temporalization, this reclamation of the right to 'inhabit time', to use historian Jean Chesneaux's expression, also modifies both our perception and our uses of space. Thanks to Jean Piaget's researches, we have become fairly well acquainted with the process of spatialization in our sensorimotor activities and, more generally, in the spatialization of our time. It's clear, however, that the inverse has not been studied so well. What do we know of the temporalization of the spaces we inhabit? To what extent does our rhythmic diversity affect our ways of existing in space? Do the architect and the urban planner give any consideration to such temporalities in their projects? How does spatial arrangement accord with temporalities that make use of it without conditioning it? Those employed in the 'manufacturing of cities' in Italy are trying to answer these questions, experimenting with various approaches. *Chronotopia* might be the offspring of Bachelard's Rhythmanalysis and his Topoanalysis or, to put it more simply, the claim to a city considered not only as a collection of structures (each with its own style, its own aesthetic, its own way of aging) and *no-man's-land*, but also as a commingling of temporalities, including what Paul Virilio has called *no-man's-time*[27]. Sandra Bonfiglioli, one of the leading theorists of chronotopian analysis who has co-edited a special issue of *Urbanistica Quaderni*[28] on the subject, seeks to bring out the feeling of temporality specific to a particular place, relying upon a 'calendar of uses' to update a site, reroute a road, build a public square etc. Many towns in Italy possess a 'Time Bureau' which, in line with the locality's move towards urbanization, plays a part in devising new urban projects. The populations that regularly frequent the city do not resemble each other and do not make use of the same aspects of time; and the better these are understood the more they can be satisfied. Guido Martinotti has divided them into four groups: residents, daily migrants, consumers and 'metropolitan businessmen'. Each one comes, according to their own rhythms, in search of something. The 'city' must respond to their various expectations and demands. Familiarity with the temporal characteristics of a city contributes to a greater habitability for everyone, according to their timetable, age, sex, use of public spaces etc. In Bolzano, Rome and Milan, the local authorities have coordinated themselves not only to harmonize their opening hours in response to the needs of their clients, but also to move eventually closer to the city's inhabitants. A public service in the depopulated heart of a historic city obliges its residents to use their cars, worsening traffic jams and pollution levels. Relocating the service in question to somewhere more accessible would appear to be a wise solution. Susanna Menichini has worked out maps for several districts in Rome, charting their temporalities: what she refers to as the spatial aspects of the politics of time. Every space, at every hour of the day and night, displays its own characteristics. These can either vary from one season to another (according to certain factors, such as tourism and the academic year) or can even cease to replicate themselves following the shift of a 'strong location' possessing a 'strong time' (such as a local service, a hospital, a business) within the tide of city-dwellers, or the construction of a new apartment block bringing a new population with it, or the opening of a branch of public transport thereby transforming the rhythm of the tides. The city is never static. Its history inscribes itself upon its architecture. Seen over this 'long duration', however, the thousands (millions?) of contrasting temporalities of the thousands (millions?) of inhabitants, not all of whom dwell in the city, become telescoped. The city's pathways correspond to precise hours of the day and night, and the urban planner cannot ignore this. His approach to spaces and locations will become temporalized, allowing him to arrange them in specific ways. No space will exist without its rhythms also being taken into account: rhythms which vary from one moment of the day to the next. No urban development will be undertaken without an awareness of a site's particular temporalities. As for the architects: they for the most part are still in favour of the absurd and restrictive division of an apartment into day use and night use. Will they invent a new room, the 'siestoir', in the same way that Georges Perec in *Species of Space* imagines a Mondoir, Tuesdoir – a room for each day of the week? Will they endow factories and office blocks with 'siesterias' right next to the cafeterias? Will they design houses by listening to their rhythms, using their vibrations and tensions as abstract – but nonetheless constructive – materials? A dwelling also rests, falls asleep and awakens. I love the moment when my house opens its eyes, sticks out its front, stretches its walls as we do our arms and then, content, settles back down upon its parcel of land. A house that takes a siesta is a house that breathes regularly, a house of communicable calm. It can even fall asleep while, all around it, lorries backfire, cars sound their horns, planes thunder and pedestrians scurry by. It's the contrast between this general commotion and the tranquillity of a house which gives the siesta its air of carefree happiness.

Outside the house, 'Time Banks' are open in the town, where customers exchange time – both their own personal time and their individual skills – as people trade produce at a market. I come to your house to babysit, and you give me English lessons. All time-based activity has a potential exchange value – to bring about such exchanges, a 'trading floor' is required. Such transactions work equally well over the Internet. Everyone profits by it. These non-commercial uses of time begin a process towards autonomy, in regard to the societal clock – the imposed timetable – and the liberating uncoupling of time from money, which constitutes a modest challenge to the prevailing economic order. People always have something to do, a task to undertake. They don't always have permanent waged work. This observation, formulated by André Gorz over twenty years ago, has only now been achieved, although this does not mean that it has been either understood or accepted: nothing could be further from the truth. To 'the revolution of elective time' we can also add 'the conquest of time to oneself'.

And what about the siesta? Have I forgotten it? No, it's still there, one proof among many of the possibility of adapting our temporalities – chronobiology, personal history, religious and communal times etc. – to those of society. The very fact that no one shares the same rhythms is a cultural value to be strengthened and allowed to bear fruit. In the face of this, it was thought for a long time that an efficient and rational society could not tolerate disorder and indiscipline. People dreamed of a permanent equilibrium (?!) and feared conflict, tension and breakdown: in short, disequilibrium. The complexity of our societies shows that equilibrium is the exception, and that we ought to think of rupture, change and 'crisis' as essential moments of renovation and renewal. The diversity of time belongs in this category. A society which obliges all of its members to breathe in time with one another, to work to the same hours and inhabit the same time is a totalitarian one, doomed to wither away. The stumbling block to most utopias is, among other things, this inability to accept diversity of behaviour and consequently to encourage all the possible combinations of temporality imaginable. Furthermore, most utopian proposals reduce the amount of time devoted to socially imposed work in order to allow its residents to educate themselves (education being, for the most part, the supreme utopian virtue), to cultivate themselves, sleep 'properly' and to rest. The majority of utopians are moralists who denounce laziness and inactivity to such an extent that they end up defending a form of puritanism. When it comes to sexuality, Charles Fourier and several other Saint-Simonists dared to break with such austerity, declaring that true liberation consisted of escaping the sombre dialectic of Good and Evil. Not by going beyond them, as Nietzsche has suggested, but by going elsewhere: taking refuge in utopia, that place which is not there, that place which is not a place, which does not offer a future but a present, meaning a present in the sense of a gift. If Thomas More reckoned the time dedicated to socially useful work to be six hours a day for the island inhabitants of *Utopia* (1516) and Campanella four hours in *The City of the Sun* (1623), the Avaïtes work five hours (*History of the Sévérambes*, attributed to Claude Gilbert, 1700) and the inhabitants of those lands imagined by Restif de la Bretonne, Jean-Baptiste

Say and Cabet hardly earned their bread by the sweat of their brow at all!

Respect and the realization of personal attraction, as postulated by Charles Fourier, liberate individuals from the (often hypocritical) restraints of morality, encouraging them to live their passions intensely for the gratification of their wishes and desires. In such a context, 'work' does not have the same presence as in our own. It's no longer work but the participation, according to one's inclinations and pleasure, in the different activities housed within Fourier's phalanstery. In such a setting, every task, even the most thankless, will find someone to carry it out, even if only once. In other words, the siesta should not be censured...

V

The Siesta Strikes Back

The siesta as a strategy for resistance? You're kidding! On whose behalf? Against what? Against 'global time', that product of the global economy which has infiltrated everywhere, shamelessly presenting itself as self-evident, self-defining and incontestable. Nevertheless, the economic system, in which everything is counted, quantified and recycled, obliges us to make use of our most precious commodity: time. Or to be more precise: daytime. Of course, there's always some angry customer screaming because the bank is closed at precisely the moment that they're free, but these days the ATMs are open twenty-four hours a day. The *elective siesta* entails a complete reorganization of timetables for both public services and businesses. It's not simply a question of closing at such and such time, but of bringing about what Pierre Sansot calls 'floating time'[29]: satisfying everyone without putting anyone out by taking the diversity of

71

individual behaviour into account. To refuse serious consideration of 'floating time' is to close one's eyes to 'unauthorized' activities: such as when I hang up a sign reading 'back soon' and then take my time returning to my post, or when I shut down my position 'temporarily', or sleep standing up and am elsewhere, all the while physically present (and physically tired). In *Manhattan Transfer* Dos Passos demonstrates the simultaneity of urban temporalities and how each person positions themselves within them. A pedestrian can always go against the flow of the crowd just as a drifter can give the impression of hurrying to a meeting while actually looking for the best route to follow without missing a single one of the city's sights. The big city, where everything functions automatically, ultimately adapts itself quite well to such transgressions. On the subject of the stroller, Pierre Sansot remarks favourably, even sympathetically, upon the zigzags, hesitations, U-turns and other diversions which endow mobility with the wanderings reminiscent of the Surrealists' celebrated 'objective chance'. The dying words of André Breton point towards our watchword: 'I seek the gold of time.' Let us humbly begin by learning how to make use of it and then venture into the mysteries of *time regained*.

The urbanization of behaviour on a planetary scale is a complex process: it simultaneously diffuses and universalizes practice, behaviour and value (in what is characterized as a move towards uniformity) while producing mixtures, crossbreeds, refusals and oppositions: unprecedented combinations which are the makings of a deviant culture. Looked at more closely, this contradiction is less oppositional than it is complementary. Before arguing the siesta's place in such a context, however, I think it might be useful to make certain things clear. Why 'the urbanization of behaviour' and not 'the globalization of capitalism' or 'the spread of cyber-culture'? To take into account the extraordinary displacement between societies which, despite everything, are contaminated by 'the globalization of markets' and 'cyber-culture' without either of them necessarily becoming integrated into an individual system whose functional logic and decision-making process remain outside their reach. In the absence of a more persuasive term, I prefer the notion of an 'urbanization of behaviour' because it conveys an active civilizing process without ascribing to it a single or unique end other than that of a 'widespread urbanization' whose frontiers and contents remain mobile. The observant reader will, of course, confirm the proliferation of an architecture which belongs everywhere, that is to say, nowhere; the identical construction, in one location after another, of huge commercial expanses or warehouses on the fringes of old towns; of highway and railroad junctions all mixed together; of urban planning that restricts itself to following a network of more or less oversized traffic systems: in short, of 'signs' that appear to be identical but which are viewed and interpreted differently by the populations of other cultures. The observant reader will, of course, fear the 'globalization of the world': that radical homogenizing of ways of living and realizing one's being over a relatively short period. The observant reader hooked up to the Internet cannot help but notice, of course, that the 'information culture' is now in competition with 'alphabetized culture' and 'popular culture'; that it's no longer simply a question of a more perfected or efficient tool, but of a whole new mental space-time, new intellectual reflexes, new ways of being with the world: of a new 'world' finally. The observant reader in front of the TV cannot, of course, ignore the – harmful – effects of television and video upon the views and opinions of the viewer; or the fact that, if television introduces the whole world into people's daily life, it does so outside the presence of the Other. Television is a non-place. It does not inform, form or transform; it does not really communicate; it makes us watch, but without connecting, reconnecting or disconnecting. Furthermore, it popularizes urbanized views on social relationships, the imagination and the natural environment. All the same, communication technology particularly suits those who make careful use of their time. In fact, the answerphone and the VCR, to take just two examples, memorize and, by extension, delay in time messages and other transmitted information. I can choose the most suitable moment in which to hear telephone messages or to watch the film or news items that have been recorded. When taking my siesta, I plug them both in and sleep peacefully...

It would be dangerous – and naïve – to ignore or underestimate these observations. But afterwards? What then? Every society in the world is being caught up in the common epic of urbanization. It reinforces the processes of exclusion even as it promotes incorporation, which is the opposite of segregation. In fact, it engenders them both without either one dominating the other, without either one hardening or becoming the norm, even for an instant. The choice, as always, is between 'civilization' and 'barbarism'. Televisual barbarism, the barbarism of 'gated' communities, of email exclusivity, of a compartmentalized world in which hate assumes the role of mediator, pitted against urban civilization, the civilization of policing, of citizenship, democratization, pacification... The choice is no longer a clear one! I lean towards the middle position, towards diversity, the pleasure of 'being', the riches of encounters, the happiness of the incomplete, of the uncertain, the haphazard, of the unstable, of the risky, the imperfect... The future should be imperfect, just as the present, our present, is often conditional and not always simple... You will have guessed, given this point of view, that the use of time is crucial, decisive. This is why the siesta is an act of resistance, an adopted position, a policy. In his rich analysis, *The Dance of Life*[30], Edward T. Hall draws upon a number of examples (Hopi, Navajo, Nuer, Quiché, Japanese,

American, European, etc.) to demonstrate at what stage time becomes fundamental to the culture of a 'people', an 'ethnicity' and a 'society'. In his eyes, time is, above all, an experience which constantly renews itself: an experience that is always singular, unique and unrepeatable. It is for this reason that he delineates the spectrum of temporal possibilities, some of which are richer than others, and dedicates himself to devising a method of classifying rhythms. The title of his study chimes well with its conclusion, arrived at after a wide anthropological survey of time: it's all about dance, that is to say, actions. Dance, ballet and choreography all set the body in motion, delimiting a space shaped by the body's movements, maintaining rhythms, indicating effort, summoning repose, flexing and relaxing muscles, imposing discipline but inviting indiscipline, liberated forms, gymnastic feats, improvised contortions, imaginative spurts... The siesta is a step, one small step in this dance. To stay with this metaphor, it's a counter-step bringing rhythm to the whole without locking it into a perpetual clock-like mechanism, a repetition, a habit. To dance one's life is to understand its rhythms, to become familiar with one's neurobiological 'timepieces', to create the 'steps' which suit our personality best, to reawaken the still, small music that plays within us all. The division of daytime into two parts (the day and the night) then into 'moments', the contents of which are dictated to us, can only countermand the sovereignty of our own temporality. To pose the siesta as a question is to question, in turn, the time we spend working.

At the end of the nineteenth century, Marx's son-in-law, Paul Lafargue set about refuting the 'right to work' hard won during the Revolution of 1848, by proposing a 'right to idleness'. It was in London, in his father-in-law's library, that Lafargue first encountered a work by Louis-Mauthurin Moreau-Cristophe (1800-1881) entitled *On the Right to Idleness and the organization of slave labour in the Greek and Roman Republics*, published in 1849 by Guillaumin and Co. He devoured the book and thought of it while composing 'The Right to Idleness'.[31] This squib was first published in the weekly journal *L'Égalité* in 1880 before appearing as a pamphlet and achieving a marked success. Considering work to be an absolute evil, Lafargue makes an apologia for idleness, arguing on behalf of a proposal made by Gotthold Lessing which he uses as his inscription: 'Let us idle over everything, except loving and drinking – and idling.' This libertarian stance finds an echo in certain of the demands made in '68, such as that for 'pleasure without restraint'. More than a century after Lafargue's call, Bruno Comby advocates the 'right to the siesta' to which I adhere, eyes shut, a signatory to the 'Siesta Charter' with which he ends his study. This comprises seven articles legitimizing the siesta (a hallowed activity, both necessary and respectable, which must not be interfered with and which everyone can practise how and when they please). Although broadening the scope of his ideas for a wider audience than the business community, I too am campaigning for a reconciliation of individuals with their rhythms and temporalities. The word 'liberty' has no real meaning without each person having control over their own time. The free use of time is the guarantee of autonomy. This individualization of time does not constitute an act of bad citizenship, a refusal to respect the 'rules' promulgated by all of life and society, a contempt for others or a falling back upon one's own creature comfort, but rather a willingness to inhabit one's own time in order to make sure of one's presence in the world, with and among other people. Availability, awareness and attentiveness are not spontaneous or regular attitudes; they gain greater substance by alternating with pauses, halts and silences. Just as sleep goes through several phases, so too are our activities cyclic. To be aware of this is good; to do what is necessary to give value to its expression is a 'labour', carried out by the self upon the self, in order that we may form a relationship with others.

Brothers and sisters! Seize the siesta!

By way of not concluding...

In the style of G.P.

Iremember: at the border between Iran and Afghanistan, on the road from Mechen to Herat, the line of buses, cars, taxis, horses and travellers waiting for the Afghani customs officials to finish their siesta in order to continue their journey.

I remember: in The Great Ummayad Mosque in Damascus, Muslims sleeping, shielded from the intense heat, taking their siesta under the protection of Allah.

I remember: my pleasure, bordering on greed, in reading books aloud to my daughter Aurélie so that she could fall into a siesta bedecked with stories and pictures. After several months of choice selections – ah! *Where The Wild Things Are* – I believed myself immured to it. Yet, despite myself, my eyes would also close and I would roll onto her narrow bed, and we would both sleep peacefully there together. This time is forever past...

I don't remember my first siesta at all.

I remember: siestas on the sandy beach at Porteaux, on the Île d'Yeu, lulled by both the rhythmic song of the sea and the babbling of the children building their improbable castles in the sand...

I remember: sleeping entwined with C. on a blue Li-Lo, after making love, in front of a blue sea tinged with green, under the blue shining sky of a Breton summer. I lick my lips again at the thought of it...

I remember: an uncomfortable siesta in an overcrowded minibus between Douala and Yaounde, packed tight – 'wedged' would be a more accurate word: a fragile piece of wood in the inflexible jaws of a steel vice – between two imposing matrons who never stopped talking.

I remember: a siesta interrupted by a mild earthquake near Van Golu in Turkey.

I remember: an impossible siesta in an open-air 'hotel' near Mokka in Yemen. Eaten alive by mosquitoes and immobilized by the thick, oppressive heat, I could barely close my eyes...

I remember: a voluptuous siesta for two, sheltered by fir trees standing to attention by the side of a tranquil swimming pool, the whole scene bathed in the scent of flowering lavender, on an isolated hillside to the west of Manosque. 'What more can you ask for?' I ended up thinking. Love shared at the beginning of the afternoon has virtues that nocturnal sexuality can never rival: the light which pleasure brings to the eyes of another...

I remember: a voluptuous siesta alone, when the afterglow drew me into a sleep populated by creatures out of a painting by Delvaux. Without any trains to catch.

I don't remember any voluptuous siestas for three or four. A lapse in my memory? But can such a number sleep so well together?

I remember: a siesta shattered by the strident ringing of the telephone. A wrong number! Curse all spoilsports of the siesta!

I remember: siestas organized like sheet music, at Albany, when, after a light and rapid meal and before the informal get-together at the end of the day, I would collapse into a deckchair by the side of the swimming pool at the middle-class motel where the university had booked a room for me. There, between sleeping and waking, I would meditate, planning my future classes. The siesta has the great merit of helping the organization of ideas, emptying the mind and resting the spirit.

I remember: a heated siesta where the sleeper, bathed in sweat like a boxer after the fight, has knocked himself out.

I remember: a holiday villa where the siesta was hardly appreciated at all, forcing me to exile myself beneath the shade of some sheltering pine trees at the bottom of the garden. Some households are extremely authoritarian and bigoted.

I remember: a particularly agreeable waking siesta during which I made a tour of the world and of all my friends. As if by telepathy.

I remember: a chrysanthemum siesta, an excuse to honour the memory of the dead.

I remember: a siesta stolen by a tableful of good friends, whom I could not – and would not – abandon.

I remember: an airborne siesta during which I could wander at my leisure, visit unknown countries and follow the cool windings of a river, mapping out the terrain of a desired sleep.

I remember so very many siestas about which I have nothing to say.

I remember: a siesta so heavily oppressive that it left a

woody aftertaste in my mouth.

I remember: a self-imposed ban on siestas: a meeting resumed through my own intervention!

I remember: an absolutely joyous siesta wrapped in a thousand pleasures. And upon waking, a flight of childish laughter.

I remember: a brief siesta, a few seconds of rare, concentrated intensity, but relaxing nonetheless.

I remember: a very long siesta which took me into a deep protective night. The day penetrating the night reminded me of rain blending with the sea.

I remember: siestas that were sugary, musical, perfumed, unlimited and joyous, while others were bitter, silent, bland, closed and constrained; or yet again, restless, upset, whimsical, the colour of flesh, wood, stone and sea; siestas that were elemental, primal and primitive; ones that were civilized and policed while others were licentious, disarrayed or suspended, sky-blue, unexpected, monastic and ecstatic: in short, a hotchpotch that was often opposed to each other as much in their effects as in their causes. The truth of the siesta always escapes us...

I remember: so many siestas that sometimes I surprise

myself as I call them to mind like one who, in search of sleep, counts sheep in order to fly with greater speed and gaiety towards the land of dreams.

1. Delumeau, J., *La civilisation de la Renaissance*, Arthaud, 1967.

2. Volume LVIII, numbers 115 and 116, 1937.

3. Numbers XVI, 1936 and XVII, 1937.

4. Bonnefoy, Y. (ed.), *Dictionnaire des mythologies*, Flammarion, 1981.

5. Le Robert, 1992.

6. Chevalier J., and Gheerbrant, *Dictionnaire des symboles*, Collection Bouqins, R Laffont, 1982.

7. Derived from Mumford, L., 'Planning for the Phases of Life', *Town Planning Review*, vol. XX, 1, 1949.

8. Mumford, ibid.

9. Thompson E.P., 'Time, Work, Discipline and Industrial Capitalism', *Past and Present* 38, 1967.

10. Texts by Jacques Le Goff consulted for this essay include 'Au Moyen Âge: Temps de l'Église et temps du marchand' (*Annales*, 1960), 'Le temps du travail dans la "crise" du XIXe siècle: du temps

médiéval au temps moderne' reprinted in *Pour un autre Moyen Âge*, Gallimard, 1977, 'Temps de travail, temps du loisir au Moyen Âge' in *Temps Libre* 1, 1980, 'Le christianisme et les rêves (IIe – VIIe siècle)' (1983 and 1985) in *L'Imaginaire médiéval*, Gallimard, 1985.

11. Thompson, ibid.

12. Giono, J., *Le poids du ciel*, Gallimard, 1949.

13. Gorz, A., *Misères du present, richesse du possible*, Gallilée, 1997.

14. Illich I., *In the Mirror of the Past: Lectures and Addresses 1978-1980*, Marion Boyars, 1992. Illich's *The Right to Useful Unemployment* (Marion Boyars, 1978) was also consulted for this essay.

15. Preface by Alexis Carrel, Plon, 1940.

16. *Les rhythmes et la vie*, Professor Laignel-Lavastine (ed.), Plon, 1947.

17. Texts by Georges Simmel consulted for this essay include 'Les grandes villes et la vie de l'esprit' in *Philosophie de la modernité*, translated into French with an introduction by J.-L. Vieillard-Baron (Payot, 1989) and 'Essai sur la sociologie des sens'

in *Sociologie et Épistémologie*, introduction by
Julien Freund (PUF, 1981).

18. Bachelard, G., *L'Intuition de l'instant*, Stock, 1931.

19. Published by the Psychological and Philosophical
Society, Rio de Janeiro, 1931.

20. Bachelard, G., *La Dialectique de la durée*, Boivin,
1936, new edition PUF, 1950.

21. Bachelard, G., *Lautréamont*, José Corti, 1939.

22. Bachelard, G., 'La Dialectique dynamique de la
rêverie mallarméenne', *Le Point*, 40-44, Souillac,
1944, reprinted in *Le Droit de rêver*, PUF, 1970.
Also by Bachelard and consulted for this essay: *La
Poétique de la rêverie* (PUF, 1960).

23. Lefebvre, H., *Éléments de rhythmanalyse*, preface
by René Lourau, Syllepse, 1992. Other texts by
Lefebvre consulted for this essay were *La Présence
et l'absence* (Casterman, 1980) and *Critique de la
vie quotidienne*, Volume 1 (Grasset, 1946),
Volume 2 (L'Arche, 1961) and Volume 3
(L'Arche, 1981).

24. Reinberg, A., 'Rhythmes scolaires et rhythmes
biologiques de l'enfant', *Universalia 1997*, p. 301-4.

Also consulted for this essay: Reinberg, A., and Ghata, J., *Les Rhythmes biologiques*, PUF, 1978.

25. Comby, B., *Éloge de la sieste*, preface by Jacques Chirac, Editions F.-X. de Guibert, 1994.

26. Mizio, F., 'L'Art de la sieste', *Libération*, 28 July-5 August, 1997.

27. Texts by Paul Virilio consulted for this essay include *La Vitesse de libération*, Galilé, 1995 and *Cybermonde, la politique du pire*, interview with Philippe Petit, *Textuel*, 1996.

28. *Urbanistica Quaderni* 'Il tempo e la citta fra natura e stroria. Altante di progetti sui tempi della citta', Sandra Bonfiglioli and Marco Mareggi (eds), Piani, Rome, 1997. Also consulted for this essay: Bonfiglioli, S., *L'Architettura del tempo. La citta multimediale* (Liguori, Napoli, 1990).

29. Sansot, P., 'Temps libre, temps flottant', *Temps Libre* 2, 1981.

30. Hall, E.T., *The Dance of Life*, Doubleday, 1984.

31. Lafargue, P., *Le Droit à la paresse* (1880), Introduction by Maurice Dommanget, Maspero, 1972.

Other works by Thierry Paquot

Les Faiseurs de nuages, essai sur la genèse des marxismes français, 1880-1914, Le Sycomore, 1980.

Homo ubanus, essai sur l'urbanisation du monde et des moeurs, Le Félin, 1990.

Henri Desroche, Mémoirs d'un faiseur de livres, interviews and correspondence with Thierry Paquot, Lieu Commun, 1992.

Vive la ville!, Arléa-Corlet, 1994.

Rêver demain. Utopie-Science-fiction-Cités idéales, (with L.Gervereau and Y.Dilas) Alternatives, 1994.

Paul-Henry Chombart de Lauwe, Un anthropologue dans le siècle, interviews with Thierry Paquot, Descartes 1996.

L'Utopie, ou l'idéal piégé, Hatier, 1996.

'L'improbable philosophie de l'art' in *Histoire des idées*, edited by Jean-Michel Besnier, Ellipses, 1996.